THE LESSON OF ST. DOMINGO:

HOW TO MAKE THE

WAR SHORT

AND THE

PEACE RIGHTEOUS.

From the "New York Tribune" of May 27, 1861.

BOSTON:
A. WILLIAMS & CO., 100 WASHINGTON ST.
1861.

THE LESSON OF ST. DOMINGO.

As the war now raging on this continent involves nearly the same elements that entered into the revolutionary history of the French part of the island of St. Domingo, the teachings of that history are unspeakably important to our government at this moment. Though the St. Domingo crucible was smaller, and the chemical ingredients perhaps a little more concentrated, the result of that experiment must in the main determine that of our grander one, except so far as we have the wisdom to modify it by varying the manipulations. No existing example of African slavery, as the basis of a European civilization, is probably quite so old as was that of St. Domingo at the time of its annihilation, and none seems, on the whole, so well fortified against change. Its was the first decisive encounter of the social forces that belong to such a state of society wherever it exists, and now that these forces have suddenly rushed into conflict here, if we are wise, we shall discard vague traditions, that may be traced back to refugee planters who threw themselves on our hospitality under Galbaud, in 1793, and verify, before believing, the histories that attribute all the "horrors" to philanthropy acting on slaves, and recognize nothing but ruin as the result.

The best sources of information in regard to the revolutionary history of St. Domingo, being French, are the least accessible. Bryan Edwards, and Rainsford, the principal English writers, deal out most of the facts that concern us at second hand, with English glosses of their own, and warped to suit an intensely pro-slavery philosophy. The details of white French eye-witnesses, such as Gen. Pamphile Lacroix, and Col. Malenfant, whose prejudices, if they had any, were not in favor of the negro, give a wholly different view of the case. The daylight which is let in by them here and there, becomes the clear and cloudless sunshine of a consistent and natural story in the work of Victor Schœlcher, published in Paris in 1843, and still more, if possible, in the much fuller history of B. Ardouin, Paris, 1855, in which every important statement is verified by ample quotations from the original documents. After a careful study of these authorities I present, as briefly as possible, an unvarnished tale of the period which is parallel to our own present crisis, and shall call particular attention to some of its points. The pride and prejudice of race and color may be great luxuries, but St. Domingo can teach us what they cost.

The French revolution of 1789 found the population of the colony of St. Domingo consisting of three classes. First, there were about* 452,000 negro slaves, chattels, whose lives were held cheap because they could easily be replaced from Africa. Second, about 40,000 whites, divided into planters and *petits blancs*, or poor whites. All whites, of pure blood, who did not own more than twenty slaves, were reckoned poor or little. Third, 28,000 mulattoes, or men of mixed blood, in whatever proportions. Their blood was considered tainted, and, though free, they had no equality with white men in the eye of the law, which carried their disabilities to such an extent, that one who presumed to strike a white of any condition, was punished by having his right hand cut off. Yet not a few of them were rich and well educated, the class having possession of one-third of the real estate of the colony, and one-fourth of the personal, including slaves. To this class belonged a few freed Africans, who were not more contemned by the whites than were the lightest mulattoes. The prejudice against color seemed to have a strength inversely proportionate to the difference of color between the parties.

For many years prior to 1789, the colonists, especially of the white proprietor class, had been aching to throw off the yoke of the mother country, and, as an independent oligarchy, to make their own laws, and administer their own affairs. Hence,

* Moreau St. Mery.

on the breaking out of the revolution in France, they at once seized the occasion to carry out their views, and established three provincial assemblies, the colony being divided into three provinces, distinguished as the North, West, and South, which in a little time nominated delegates to a general colonial convention, to meet at St. Marc. Thus the white slaveholders initiated the insular revolution. The mulattoes, however, were not uninterested nor without hope from what was going on in France, that they would share the blessings of political reform. The spirit of the white planters was soon manifested to be very different from that of the revolutionists in the mother country. The latter, by a decree of the National Assembly, March 8, 1789, had in favor of mulattoes expressly accorded political privileges to all free persons over twenty-five years of age, who were proprietors in the colonies. And they had also, in an abstract way, August 20, 1789, declared that "all men are born, and continue, free and equal as to their rights." But neither of these decrees having yet reached the colony in an official form, on the second of November, 1789, Lacombe, a mulatto, in a written petition addressed to one of the aforesaid provincial assemblies of white planters, requested that his class might enjoy the benefit of this declaration of the rights of man, and be represented in the assembly. They voted his petition incendiary, and hung him! This was the first victim and the first "horror." Seventeen days after, Ferrand de Beaudiere, a white man, of seventy years, who held an inferior judicial office, for the crime of drawing up for some colored men a memorial similar to that of Lacombe, was lynched and decapitated. This was the second victim and the second "horror." The convention at St. Marc proceeded at once to set at defiance the special decree of the National Convention in favor of the free men of the colonies, which had now reached the colony officially, and went further to declare themselves independent of the mother country, and to assert that they acted by the authority of their constituents, and not of the National Assembly. More than that, they proceeded to *seize the magazine at Leogane.* The governor, Peynier could not tolerate these usurpations, and there resulted two governments. The national guard was divided, part serving the governor and part the planters' assembly of St. Marc.. The latter stuck red pompons on their caps, the former adhered to the white, and the two factions took the names of *pompons rouge* and *pompons blancs* from this circumstance. The planters' assembly called the governor to their bar to give an account of himself. He came and pronounced their dissolution, ordering Col. Mauduit to disperse them, which he did after an obstinate resistance, and the loss of fifteen men, carrying off the flag of the *pompons rouge.* The desperate planters then offered to arm the free colored men, but on terms so degrading, that they were not accepted. The mulattoes preferred to serve the side of the mother country, as had also the *petits blancs* and most of the professional men. They offered to bear arms under the governor, but here the prejudice of color came in, and they could not be allowed to wear the white pompon of the French service, but must be distinguished by a *yellow* one. They returned the arms they had already received, and took a neutral position.

The revolutionary quarrel between the pure whites continued to the 23d October, 1790, without any active interference from the free colored class, or any sign of interest on the part of the slaves. At the latter date, Vincent Ogé, a young mulatto who had been residing in France for his education, landed furtively at the Cape, without troops or arms. He put himself at the head of two or three hundred of his class in arms, and made a modest demand upon the planters' assembly of the North, of the legal rights of his class. In this address he took care to say, "I shall not have recourse to any raising of the slave gangs;" "I never comprehended in my claims the negroes in a state of slavery;" and "Our adversaries are not merely unjust to us, but to themselves, for they do not seem to know that *their interests are one with ours.*" The planters gave him very little time to concentrate the strength that belonged to his cause. They rushed on him with an overwhelming force, and drove all whom they did not slay into the Spanish part of the island. The refugees were given up by the Spanish governor, who only asked the cross of St. Louis as the reward of his treachery! The punishment of these modest mulattoes is worthy of particular mention, since, of all the horrors afterwards perpetrated by colored or black man, there was none to exceed it, and there had been nothing on the part of the colored or black men to provoke it. Of the prisoners, the white assembly formally condemned thirteen to the galleys, twenty-two to be gibbeted, and two—Ogé and his lieutenant, Chavannes—to have their arms, legs, thighs and hips broken alive on the wheel, upon a scaffold, and then to live in their torments with their faces towards heaven, in presence of all beholders, as long as God should spare their lives. The white assembly attended in a body to witness the spectacle, and the heads of the victims, after their death, were paraded on poles and made as public as possible. This was on the 25th of February, 1791.

In the meantime the French National Assembly had approved the stand taken by the colonial governor, and ordered two battalions of troops to be sent to his aid. Unfortunately, the partisans of the assembly of St. Marc, who in great numbers had been driven to France by the governor, found an opportunity to corrupt the troops, while they were in the harbor of Brest. So when they landed in St. Domingo, in spite of Blanchelande, Peynier's successor, they took part with the planters, and mounted the *pompon rouge*. The planters managed also to seduce the members of Col. Mauduit's regiment, and to attract by their gold and their condescension, the *petits blancs*, and, like our present secessionists, they raised an army of white vagabonds, whom they supported by levying heavy taxes. A planter by the name of Boré, who wrote on the troubles of the time, complains that he had to pay a tax of two thousand *livres*, though he owned but twenty-one slaves. The consequence of all this was, that the provisional assembly of the West resumed its sittings, and called on Col. Mauduit to restore the flag which he carried off when he dispersed them. Mauduit, having no means of resistance, started at the head of his demoralized regiment, on the 4th of March, 1791, to restore the flag. On the way he was not only assailed and massacred by the white mob mixed with French and colonial soldiers, but his corpse was hacked in pieces and borne in triumph into the city. Among the mutilators was said to be Madame Martin, a white lady, who afterwards enjoyed the hospitality of the United States.

The power of the mother country in the colony died, for the time, with Mauduit. Blanchelande became a fugitive, and a rich planter, named Caradeux, a monster of cruelty not surpassed by any of the black ones in the succeeding years, became ruler of the colony and Captain General of the National Guard, if there could be said to be any ruling where all was anarchy. Such a power, of course, did not stand firmly. The *petits blancs*, though now acting under the slaveholders, were clamorous for their own rights, and had actually murdered two rich planters, who were obnoxious to them, and carried about their heads on poles. The rich mulattoes were talking between their teeth about their political rights, and in fact entering into a deep conspiracy in the neighborhood of Port au Prince. Some of the white planters, especially near the Cape, were still anti-revolutionary, and wished to restore Blanchelande and adhere to their allegiance to France. It is said that they began to talk about using their human chattels in a military way to promote their political purposes, and that this sort of conversation falling on the ears of Toussaint, a confidential slave, the coachman of M. Bayon de Libertas, was the spark which kindled the first servile insurrection. Whether or not the planters did have any such communication, as is asserted, with Toussaint, Boukman, Jean Francois, Jeannot Bullet and Biassou, certain it is that those slaves made a pretty extensive conspiracy to assert their own liberty, and considering their own slender means and slight knowledge, and the utter ignorance of the masses on which they operated, they did it with wonderful adroitness. Whether they had seen the "glittering generality," put forth by the National Assembly two years before, is not known, but they professed to have a decree for their general liberation, which they caused to be read in their assembly by a young mulatto pressed into that service. They carefully arranged their conspiracy, sanctifying it, as it is said, with religious ceremonies partly African and partly Christian. The sacrifice of a black pig was the African part, and for the Christian part a hymn in the patois of the negroes is on record, the sentiment of which would certainly do no discredit to King David or Dr. Watts.

Though it was with the utmost difficulty that the few leading negroes above named persuaded their brethren to commit themselves to an insurrection, when committed, they were too eager, and by mistaking the instructions, some of them commenced several hours too early. This put the whites on their guard. Nevertheless, on the dawn of August 23, 1791, as had been agreed, a very extensive revolt took place in the neighborhood of Cape Francois, which resulted in the slaughter of 2,000 whites and mulattoes on one side, and about 10,000 blacks on the other. It was led bravely by Boukman, who was slain fighting, after which his followers fled before the National Guard, and were butchered like sheep. Before they were checked, the blacks showed in what school they had studied their lesson, by sticking upon poles the heads of three hundred whites, at the very spot where the whites had stuck up the heads of Ogé and Chavannes. Yet it is credibly related that one of the insurgent slaves by the name of Bartholo, in the midst of the carnage, at the risk of his own life, bore his master, one Mongin, to a place of safety. After the insurrection was crushed, Bartholo was condemned to death on the information of the very (white) man whose life he saved.

All classes of whites and mulattoes joined in suppressing this insurrection, and pushed their advantage of science and arms so far, that they over-did it. By their wholesale slaughter of slaves who had no part in the conspiracy they widely roused the black population in all quarters and pressed thousands of them to fly to the mountains, where they were organized in bands under Jean Francois, Biassou and other chiefs, who soon learned how to direct their energies efficiently.

After their common peril was abated, the whites and mulattoes at once fell into a bloodier quarrel than before. The whites swore they would not yield an iota of privilege to the "bastard race." The mulattoes armed to take their legal rights by force, and this time they fought so prosperously, that their antagonists were humbled and obliged to make a treaty of peace in which they acknowledged that the execution of Ogé was a crime, and awarded to the mulattoes all the rights they claimed.

In this last passage at arms, known as the battle of *Croix-des-Bouquets*, both the white and mulatto planters employed as auxiliaries armed slaves, who behaved with great valor on both sides. These auxiliaries were called *Swiss*, and in making the treaty of peace, the white planters contended that these men having become accustomed to freedom it would not be safe to send them back to the plantations, or to suffer them to remain in the colony, to which the mulattoes, in spite of their kinship agreed. So it was stipulated that they should be colonized (without wives or families,) to Honduras, with agricultural implements and provisions for three months. They were put on board a ship to the number of 300, and commissioners to superintend their settlement were appointed to go with them. The commissioners, however, probably by the contrivance of the whites, sailed in another vessel, and the two vessels were separated the first night. The captain who had the *Swiss* for passengers proceeded to Jamaica and offered them all for sale. The remonstrance of the victims spoiled their market, the inhuman wretch then put to sea and landed them all on a desert key with scanty provisions. Before they were quite starved a passing vessel reported their case to the English Admiral at Port Royal, and he had them conveyed back to St. Domingo. The Colonial Assembly received them, and put them in irons on board a vessel in the harbor of St. Nicolas Mole. They had not been there long before assassins were sent on board, who shutting the captain in his cabin, selected sixty of the strongest of the *Swiss*, knocked them on the head, and threw them overboard. The rest were left in their chains, as victims to a pestilential disease, which is said to have been purposely communicated, and all but twenty or thirty perished.

The peace so sealed with blood was soon broken. The whites again spurned the mulattoes, and invited the Governor of Jamaica to seize the colony for the English. He refused this time, to accept by and by. The war of color raged on, and the revolted negro chiefs in the mountains somewhat strengthened themselves. A set of civil commissioners was sent from France to make peace but effected nothing. The city of Port-au-Prince was half burned in a savage quarrel that grew out of a personal fight between a free black and a white soldier, and the whites, to satisfy their revenge on the mulattoes, to whom they attributed the mischief, committed an awful massacre on their wives and children. The loss of property at Port-au-Prince in a single day is estimated by Lacroix at fifty million francs. The mulattoes, aided by the brave young negro, Hyacinth, and a band of revolted slaves, took a terrible vengeance again at the Croix-des-Bouquets.

It was in this state of things that, in September, 1792, a new set of civil commissioners, Sonthonax, Polverel and Ailhaud, arrived at the Cape. They had left France just before the dethronement of Louis XVI., were accompanied by 6,000 troops, which added to those already in the island, would make their force about 14,000, and had the amplest legal powers, Up to their appointment, the authorities sent from France to the colony had been satisfactory to the *Club Massiac;* that is. decidedly pro-slavery. But these commissioners were Girondists, and in favor with the *Amis des Noirs*, who were theoretically opposed to slavery. This gave the alarm to the Massiac Club, which took immediate measures to invite the English and deliver the colony to them. The instructions of the commissioners, however, confined them to the enforcement of the laws, specially including that for securing political equality to free men of all colors, and enjoined upon them "the repression of the seditious movements of the slave-gangs." There was not the slightest squinting towards emancipation in any circumstances. The French government, in fact, as represented in these instructions, maintained towards slavery in the colony precisely the same policy as that now maintained by our Federal administration towards slavery in the disturbed States. And the commissioners, of whom Polverel and Sonthonax were distinguished French lawyers, like Gen. Butler, at once offered their services to suppress servile insurrection. More than that, they indignantly repelled the accusation of the *Club Massiac* that they were going to emancipate slaves, and conceded that no power but the colonial assembly could act in regard to the slaves. Polverel declared that if the national assembly were to legislate any change whatever in the condition of their "movable property," *he* would abdicate his mission on the spot; and Sonthonax and Ailhaud went further to say, or rather to swear, if the national assembly should ever become so fanatical as to pronounce the abolition of slavery, they would oppose it with all their might.

These commissioners in their opening proclamation commenced with these words: "Invariably attached to the laws we come to see them executed; we declare in the name of the mother-country, of the national assembly and of the king, that we shall henceforward recognize but two classes of men in the colony of St. Domingo, the free, without any distinction of color, and the slaves." They accordingly received into their army the troops of mixed blood, suppressed the *pompons rouges* and Caradeux, and made themselves particularly active everywhere in recapturing and resubjugating *the revolted slaves*. Some of this work, too, was horribly bloody. They filled the prisons of Cape Francois with recovered runaways to the number of four or five hundred! This splendid slave-hunting, this sublime "soundness on the goose," however, did not satisfy all the white planters. Some of them were so turbulent that the civil commissioners were obliged to put them on board the fleet, along with the corrupted troops that had helped murder Colonel Mauduit, to be sent to France. Just at this crisis, the malcontents were rejoiced at the arrival of General Galbaud from France, a planter of the colony, of the *pompon rouge* party, who had got himself appointed governor in the place of Blanchelande. It was falsely supposed that his power was superior to that of the commissioners. But the latter soon obliged him to confess that he had obtained his office in contravention of a law that forbade any man to be governor who owned an estate in the colony, by concealing the fact. He, too, was sent to the fleet to be conveyed to France. But while the fleet was lying in the harbor, a quarrel occurred between a white naval officer and a mulatto on the quai. The officer called on the commissioners to punish the mulatto, who refused to do it without a fair hearing of the case. This was seized upon by Galbaud and the gentlemen and lady planters on board the fleet, as the means of rousing the sailors and soldiers on board to vengeance, and Galbaud's brother, at the head of two or three thousand armed men, landed and attacked the commissioners in the government palace. Their whole available force for defence, including regulars, mulattoes, and a few free blacks, scarcely amounted to five hundred. These defended them bravely through the first day, and drove the sailors back to the ships, but achieved little hope for the certain contest of the next day. The brains of the two lawyers, under the awful pressure of circumstances which they could no longer control, during that night produced a dispatch or circular to the revolted negro chiefs, then hovering in the vicinity, in which we see the first gleam of good sense that appears in their conduct. They began with these remarkable words: "We declare that it is the will of the French Republic and that of its delegates, to give liberty to all the negro warriors who will fight for the Republic, under the orders of the civil commissioners," &c. They proceeded to promise the alleviation of slavery, and final emancipation to other slaves who would continue to work and behave well, and added, "All the slaves who shall be declared free by the delegates, shall be the equals of the white men, and those of all other colors. They shall enjoy all the rights pertaining to French citizens."

Having dispatched this call for aid, the commissioners awaited the attack, which was resumed with still greater force, under Galbaud in person, at day-break. By eleven o'clock the commissioners were obliged to retire to a strong-hold in the suburbs, and Galbaud remained master of the palace. The thousands of sailors not content with this victory, commenced plundering the city. The wine-vaults falling first in their way, put them in a condition fit for havoc, and the pillage was soon turned into an indiscriminate slaughter. There was soon added to this a horrible fact, which illustrates the wisdom of the costly operations for reducing the revolted slaves. The prisons were opened, and the hundreds of captives, maddened by a sense of wrong, were let loose on the scene. Who did it, no one knew; some attributed it to the city slaves, and some to the commissioners, who in their report denied it. The released prisoners joined the sailors in their bloody work, as did many of the city slaves. Others nobly endeavored to save the families of their masters. The negro chiefs, who had been, as we have seen, invited in under the direction of the commissioners and the mulatto officers, drove off the sailors and plundering blacks, rescued many white citizens and aided in saving a large amount of property. Galbaud and many of the white planters escaped to the fleet, not a few being drowned in their haste to embark. A large part of perhaps the richest city of its size in the world was laid in ashes. Lacroix says the day's work cost a hundred millions of francs.

It was a very sharp corner which the representatives of the grandest power in Europe turned on that occasion. A few weeks before, they had been chasing fugitive slaves with their army, scattered for that purpose in all quarters, and cutting off the ears, and branding the left shoulders of all they could catch, with the letter M. (*marron*), as a peace offering to propitiate the slaveholders; now they were reporting to their government that "the new citizens, (the slaves,) have showed an unheard of courage and intrepidity; in the midst of murder, carnage and fire, they gave their ancient tyrants an example of humanity, of philanthropy. While one part of these men was fighting the sailors, the other was occupied in patroling the streets, gathering the frightened whites and conveying them, protected from insults, into the camp of the civil commissioners, where we furnished them lodgings and provisions." This was the compliment they were obliged to pay to the revolted black slaves, who at their request saved their lives from the very slave masters whose humble hounds they had made themselves. Bryan Edwards says they invited in these revolted negro chiefs by promising them their liberty and the *plunder of the city*. Unfortunately for that assertion we have the proclamation on which they came, which promises nothing but liberty and citizenship, and the testimony of both white and mulatto slaveholders that their conduct was most exemplary.

After his remarkable repulse, Galbaud, with a large part of the fleet, sailed for the United States, carrying with him a great number of white planters, who had been the greatest pests of the colony. The commissioners had dispersed and nearly used up their army in the work of putting down anti-revolutionary white cabals on one side and negro revolts on the other. They were threatened with invasion from the Spanish part of the island and from England. On the 10th of July, 1793, they wrote to the national assembly, giving a report of the above events at the Cape. "Such, citizen representatives, is the disastrous position in which Galbaud has left us in the province of the North. Without a navy, without money, without the means of procuring any, and with provisions for only one month, yet we do not despair of the safety of the country. We are going on; we do not ask of you ships nor sailors; it is with the *natives of the country*, that is, *the Africans*, that we shall save to France the property of St. Domingo."

Thus had it been beaten into their politic heads that a better use could be made of the half million black people, over whom the fifty thousand white and yellow pretended proprietors had been fighting, than cutting off their ears, printing M's on their skins with hot iron, and keeping them subservient chattels to the said proprietors.

Many of the more moderate and reasonable white slaveholders began to be of the same opinion. The national assembly had so enlarged the powers of the civil commissioners that they could act on the question of slavery, according to their own interpretation of their instructions, if it became necessary. But almost immediately after the troubles of the Cape, before they could act in concert, they were obliged to separate, Polverel going to the West. There he found the Spaniards exerting such an influence on the revolted slaves, that without waiting for the concurrence of Sonthonax (Ailhaud had returned to France) he issued a proclamation on the 27th August, 1793, giving not only liberty to all revolted slaves who would return to labor, but, by a sort of agrarian law, dividing among them the estates of planters that had become *vacant*. The same provision was made for slaves who had borne or should bear arms for the Republic, and ultimate liberty and landed provision was promised to all other slaves. This action was confined to the province of the West, but encouragement was given that if should soon be extended to the other provinces. Equally without concert, the younger and more radical Sonthonax, on the 29th of August, proclaimed his decree of emancipation for the province of the North. His decree gave universal liberty, but made no landed provision. It provided a detailed plan for securing industry and order. This very successful document quoting from the then most recent French Declaration of human rights, commenced thus: "*Men are born and continue free and equal in their rights;* such, citizens, is the gospel of France; it is more than time it were proclaimed in all the departments of the Republic." It then proceeds to state, what the commissioners had before publicly and solemnly denied, that the commission was sent not only to secure the equality of the free, but to prepare gradually for the general enfranchisement of the slaves, and to plead the most funny and ingenious excuses for having sustained slavery, as we have seen they did. The emancipation was afterwards made universal in the West, and completed by a proclamation of Polverel in the province of the South, October 31, 1793.

After the last chain was broken there were no "horrors," except those which necessarily arose from the English invasion, invited by the rebel planters. The planters who remained in the colony, faithful to France, found no difficulty in carrying on their plantations prosperously with the hired labor of their former slaves. After two months trial of freedom in the North and West, Polverel, the distinguised veteran, cool and sagacious Parisian lawyer, has these remarkable words in his above mentioned proclamation of liberty for the South.

"Two years of war against the insurgent Africans had convinced the proprietors that it was thenceforth impossible to maintain slavery. Their works were deserted, their houses and their plantations were burned and laid waste. France poured out men and money; and while her armies were annihilated in St. Domingo, those of the Africans were recruited every day by new desertions from the slave-gangs. The colonist despaired of ever seeing his land restored to value, because he knew of no culture but that of slaves.

"The delegates of the Republic presented to the Africans the idea and hope of general liberty, a certainty of a living to the warriors, and a share in the produce to the cultivators; this word sufficed to create soldiers for the Republic, to reëstablish order, to re-people the workshops and reanimate industry. The proprietors, astonished at this prodigy (for it was such to them), voluntarily, and with a spirit of generous rivalry, gave liberty to the Africans who had till then been under their control. They even entreated the civil commission to hasten as much as possible the declaration of general liberty, and the publication of the regulations which the new order of things demanded."

Just after this, the British Government, that never does things by the halves, landed an invading army. The effort to make St. Domingo a British colony was continued about five years, cost Great Britain about one hundred millions of dollars, and forty-five thousand lives, and finally she had the honor of being expelled from the island by black and mulatto troops under a pure black general-in-chief.

Under that chief, the born statesman who probably planned the first slave insurrection, of August 23, 1791, the colony *was saved to France.* Under his wise, though rather despotic civil administration from 1796 to 1802, the colony, to use the language of the French General Lacroix, "marched as if by enchantment towards its ancient splendor." Though the laboring population by the slaughters and famines of war had been reduced to less than four hundred thousand, and the productive capital, other than land, had been mainly annihilated, the exports of one of Toussaint's best years compare with those of a year in the palmiest period of slavery, in regard to three principal items, as follows:—

	Under Slavery.	Under Toussaint.
Sugar, ...	145,192,043 lbs.	53,400,000 lbs.
Coffee, ...	71.663,187 lbs.	34,370,000 lbs.
Cotton, ...	6,698,858 lbs.	4,050,000 lbs.

This is pretty well for a colony that was "utterly ruined" by emancipation.

How all this was lost to France by Napoleon's costly attempt to restore slavery, is of no further importance to our present purpose, than as it proves that the spirit of liberty, once aroused in black men, is no more temporary or evanescent than in white ones.

What is the lesson of this history? Is it not this? Negro slaves, ignorant, contented, jolly, cowardly, passive as they may be, can be educated to insurrection in such a school as the two very different governments at Washington and Montgomery are now establishing, and probably will be.

Though both these governments should at first agree perfectly in ignoring the negro, and even join their forces to suppress "seditious movements" of slaves, one or the other will at last be obliged to recognize black men as a raw material of military power. Though the black material may be very raw, under proper guidance, it may soon be made very effective, *on either side.*

Had the French commissioners when they first landed in St. Domingo, instead of proclaiming their purpose to reduce the slaves to subjection, and keep them subject, made the proclamation which they did one year after, they would have saved some ten thousand white and thirty thousand colored lives, they would have saved the capital city from conflagration, and their own consistency from shipwreck. It cost all that to sacrifice the principles of the revolution in the mother country to a temporary supposed expediency in the colony.

Slave insurrections are easily put down for the time, but when they occur while the country is disturbed and excited by war, they can never fail to increase the chance of success in a subsequent rising, by the experience which those who are sure to escape will have acquired. There was really but one regular slave insurrection in St. Domingo, and that was promptly suppressed; but out of it grew at least four able guerilla chiefs, and one accomplished military leader, whom Bonaparte could conquer only by falsehood and perfidy.

Nobody who understands the world, expects that the magnanimity, or sense of justice, or regard for the fundamental principles of Christianity, in the people who are now engaged in a life or death struggle to sustain the government of their choice —sentiments and principles that have not been strong enough in peace even to cause them to apply a file to the roughness of the negro's chain—will now, in time of war, impel them to apply the cold chisel. But if they will not have the manhood, self-respect, "fanaticism," or whatever else it may be, to gratify a sense of justice, and wipe off a blot of inconsistency from the beloved institutions of the country, will they have the pure folly not to sacrifice a little prejudice of race and complexion, if at that cost they can effect a speedy and favorable solution of the difficulty?

If we have not justice or philanthropy enough to do spontaneously what France was *obliged* to do for St. Domingo, ought we not to have *wit* enough? Nations are saved, after all, only by their *wits*. The Yankee nation has saved itself from poverty by its wits. In its own geographical domain, it has wit enough not to work against the grain of nature, but with it. Wind, water, fire, foreigners,—men, animals, vegetables and minerals, all free in their way, but all have to work for the Yankee. Yankees have tastes, loves and hates, more perhaps, than they can give good reasons for. But who ever heard of a live Yankee sawing his boards and grinding his corn by hand, because he thought the stream running by his door, coming out of a peat bog, too black to be beautiful?

We are firm believers, as at present advised, in the intellectual and physical superiority of the white "race" over the black, ethnologically speaking. But the great Spirit of the Universe, who delights in varieties, contrasts, parallel differences, rainbows, succession, wave after wave, and all that, is always stronger than any *one* "race," no matter how pert and proud of itself. When he is going to raise any thing particularly high, he likes to begin mighty low. Witness in the old Roman slave-market stupid natives of Britain, hardly worth selling. His law for all races is, to baptize their infant greatness in insurrection. So he did our special Yankee race at Lexington and Bunker Hill. So he did the ebon brothers that for more than half a century have held the most toothsome island on the globe against the whole white "race," including the very slave-power which has ruled *us* all that time, and against which we have only just rebelled. Is it not about time to expect a baptism of blood for the four millions of the same race on this continent, when it has manifestly already cost the conversion of several millions of white men into devils, to hold them to the condition of brutes? If the blood must flow, why not regulate the flow?

If the white race has not yet reached the summit-level between its growth and its decay, it is because it will, in the main, as it has begun to do, place itself in line with the universe, in regard to God's favorite principle of tolerating and encouraging variety in unity. But if the Yankee branch, in spite of its *e-pluribus-unum* professions, is going to persist in the old chopping-and-stretching-all-men-to-one-bedstead experiment, if it is bound not to recognize any manhood below the zero of the dye-house, it will soon pass into history as a sapless, dry, rotten limb, be blown off, and only those who may know the meaning of *knots*, will know that it ever existed.

To recur to the lesson. Our Federal Government is situated, in regard to our present controvery, very much as France was in St. Domingo, represented by its civil commissioners. England is still more interested in our quarrel than she was in theirs, but in a position to make her play a very different role. She wants no slaves, but she wants cotton, and has no prejudice against color. Indeed she is never better suited than when she is surrounded by the largest possible proportion of free black folks. Suppose, with the utmost dignity and grandeur, we persist in the policy, which failed after the fairest trial under Sonthonax and Polverel, the policy of adhering with self-sacrificing magnanimity to the constitutional view of slavery which has brought all the trouble on us, and disdaining to make any use of the negro, except to offer him up, when caught revolting, as a propitiatory sacrifice to the demon of secession, till the united forces of Jeff. Davis's "white trash" in arms, Virginia sedge, yellow fever, hope deferred and other natural causes have worn off the edge of our enthusiasm, the soles of our shoes, and the seats of our trowsers, the pockets having become empty, what will prevent the English at that juncture from taking the quarrel off our hands, invading the cotton States and doing just what Sonthonax and Polverel did to drive them out of St. Domingo? They probably learned some wisdom in that affair. If they do it, and convert the Southern States into a Southern Canada, we shall be at least no worse off than we have been, probably far better, and the slave States will be infinitely better off. But is that the best thing which we northern children of '76, and our regenerated Federal Government, rejoicing in the unanimous loyalty of nineteen out of the thirty-four States can do?

Gentle reader, don't suppose me insensible to the intense whisper which has been, all this while, buzzing into my ears from a million voices—" Policy! policy! policy! especially in war—don't for goodness gracious sake, spoil the majesty of this unanimous northern enthusiasm, or drive into open secession the ticklish Unionists of the Border States." All I have to reply is, " Spit the meal out of your mouths. In times that try men's souls hypocrisy is not always particularly useful. If Gov. Magoffin and the witty Prentice are not secessionists at heart, plain common sense won't hurt either of them. The Federal Executive is the lawgiver in the rebel States, in the time of rebellion, and cannot shirk that responsibility. He represents a government which was designedly created without the organs to recognize any human being as a chattel. As long as the Federal Government represented by him gives unjust and foolish laws, the rebels can fight with good courage, believing that the black people will remain neutral or quiet, and *knowing* that their Maker, who will vindicate the good sense of his own workmanship, cannot take sides with those who treat that workmanship as a contemptible botch, not worth using at a pinch. A sensible proclamation from the Federal Executive setting forth that *all* the inhabitants of the rebel States, who will be loyal, shall be, and be treated as, citizens of the United States, would paralyze the rebels worse than the four Hebrew words did Belshazzar, and prove to all sensible men at the South that they can safely trust us, because we are not simpletons, Pecksniffs and sneaks, as they had always been obliged to believe."

ELIZUR WRIGHT.

BOSTON, 13 *Avery Street*, May 22, 1861.

APPENDIX.

Proclamations of Polverel and Sonthonax.

The Proclamation of Polverel, dated August 27, 1793, only conferred or rather confirmed a partial liberty, and promised to moderate the slave code and raise the slaves nearly to the level of freed men, as witness the following articles extracted from it:—

ART. 1. All Africans or descendants of Africans, of every sex and age, who will remain on, or return to, the estates to which they have heretofore belonged, which estates have been or shall be declared vacant in pursuance of my proclamation of the 21st of this month, are declared free, and shall enjoy, from the present time, all the rights of French citizens, on the sole condition of their engaging to continue to work in the cultivation of the said estates.

3. All the negroes hitherto in a state of insurrection or revolt, and also the independent negroes who inhabit the *Maniel* (or Bahoruco), or other places in the Spanish part of St. Domingo, shall have the benefit of the provisions of Art. 1.

8. The whole of the vacant estates in the province of the West shall belong in common, to all the warriors of said province and all the cultivators of said vacant estates, in the proportions which shall be hereafter determined.

9. The estates shall remain undivided during the war and the internal troubles, till the time which shall be indicated in Art. 24; the revenues of them shall be paid into the treasury of the administration; a responsible treasurer shall render an account of them each year, and shall distribute to each his share, according to the proportions indicated by the preceding article, and those which shall be hereafter.

12. Every creditor, present or absent, who shall not present his claim within one year at most, is non-suited.

24. There shall be no process of partition of estates declared vacant, among the new proprietors, until after a total valuation of the debts, principal and interest.

37. There shall be admitted to this partition, as warriors, all the armed negroes who are actually in a state of insurrection, who will restore to the Republic, or aid in restoring to its possession the aforesaid territories before being obliged by force of arms to do so, who will take the oath of fidelity to the Republic, and who will fight for it to the end of the foreign war and the internal troubles.

38. Liberty shall be irrevocably acquired by them, by the sole act of releasing the territory and taking the oath of fidelity to the Republic; the obligation to bear arms in future, in the service of the Republic, being imposed upon them only as a necessary condition of being admitted to a share of the land as warriors, they can be permitted to become cultivators whenever they relinquish the

military profession, provided they fulfil the conditions above prescribed to cultivators.

39. All the real estate belonging to the crown of Spain, to its nobles, monks and priests, of which the republic shall make conquest, shall in the same manner be divided between the warriors in the service of the republic in St. Domingo, and the workmen or cultivators who shall engage themselves in its cultivation.

40. All Spanish and all African insurgents, either fugitive slaves (marrons) or independent, and all other individuals of whatever nation they may be, who shall have assisted the arms of the Republic, and who shall have contributed to facilitate its conquest of the Spanish part, shall be admitted to the partition, as French warriors.

41. All armed citizens of the province of the West, who shall remain for home defence, shall also be admitted to the partition, the same as their brethren in arms who shall go to conquer the eastern part of the island.

42. All the fugitive Africans (marrons), insurgent or independent, as well as all the slaves of the Spanish Crown, of the nobles, and of the Spanish monks and priests, who will apply themselves to the cultivation of the land, shall be declared free, French citizens, and admitted to a share in the lands aforesaid, as cultivators.

43. There shall, moreover, be observed, in the partition of the lands aforesaid of the crown, nobles, monks and priests, all the provisions of my preceding proclamation, relative to the partition of lands declared vacant in the province of the West.

44. In case the civil commission should decide to extend this Proclamation to the provinces of the North and the South, the estates declared vacant shall be taken in one mass for the three provinces, and the warriors and cultivators of the French part shall be admitted, without distinction of provinces, to share among them the totality of the said estates declared vacant, and the proceeds of the same, according to the order and conditions which have just been prescribed for the province of the West.

The Proclamation of Sonthonax, dated August 29, 1793, contained the following Articles:—

ART. 1. The declaration of the rights of man and of the citizen, [that of the French National Assembly,] shall be printed, published, and posted in all needful places.

2. All the negroes and mixed-bloods now in slavery are declared free to enjoy all the rights attached to the quality of French citizens; they shall, however, be subject to the regulations contained in the following articles:—

5. Domestics, of either sex, shall be engaged for the service of their masters or mistresses only for three months, and that for wages to be fixed on by mutual agreement.

6. The heretofore slaves, domestics, attached to the service of persons over sixty years of age, to invalids, to children at nurse or under ten years, shall not be at liberty to quit that service. Their wages remain fixed at eight dollars (gourdes), per month, for nurses, and forty-eight dollars per annum for others, without distinction of sex.

9. The negroes at present attached to the estates of their former masters shall be bound to remain on them; they shall be employed in the cultivation of the soil.

10. The enrolled warriors who serve in the army or in the garrison, shall have the right to become employed as cultivators on the estates, by previously obtain-

ing permission from their commander, or an order from us, which cannot be given without a volunteer to supply the place vacated.

11. The heretofore slave cultivators shall be engaged for one year, during which time they cannot change from the estate without permission of the justice of the peace.

12. The revenues of each estate shall be divided into three equal portions, after deducting the taxes, which shall be levied on the whole. One-third appertains to the ownership of the soil, and shall belong to the proprietor. He shall have the benefit of another third for the expenses of management. The remaining third shall be divided among the cultivators, in the manner hereinafter provided.

10. The cultivators, moreover, shall have their *provision patches*, which shall be assigned equitably, having regard to the quality of the soil, and the quantity which will be sufficient for each.

26. The Inspector-General of the province of the North will be charged to inspect all the estates, and to put the justices of the peace in possession of the fullest possible information as to the order and discipline of the laboring forces, and to report on the same to us and to the Governor and Attorney-General. He shall be on duty at least twenty days in each month.

27. The correction of the *whip* is absolutely suppressed; in its place shall be substituted, for faults against discipline, the *bar* for one, two, or three days, according to the exigency of the case. The severest penalty shall be the loss of a part or the whole of the wages.

28. In regard to civil misdemeanors, the heretofore slaves shall be judged as other French citizens.

29. Cultivators shall not be obliged to labor on Sunday.

31. Pregnant women, in the seventh month, shall not work in the field, and shall not return to such work till two months after their confinement.

32. Cultivators shall be able to leave the estate on account of health or from manifest incompatibility of character, or on demand of the gang in which they are employed. All such cases shall be submitted to the justice of the peace, assisted by his assessors.

33. Fifteen days after the promulgation of this proclamation, all men who have no property, and who shall not be enrolled, or attached to cultivation, or employed in domestic service, and who shall be found wandering, shall be arrested and imprisoned.

Another article extends the same to women, and another provides that this imprisonment shall extend to one month for the first offence, three for the second, and twelve, on public works, for the third.

36. Persons attached to cultivation and domestics, shall, on no pretext, leave the commune where they reside, without the permission of the municipality.

www.ingramcontent.com/pod-product-compliance
Lightning Source LLC
LaVergne TN
LVHW011145110826
845150LV00008B/2521

* 9 7 8 1 4 1 8 1 9 1 8 9 4 *